Dedication

I would like to dedicate this book to the people who have stood by me throughout my life. A deep thank you to my family: my mom and dad; my wife, Angie; my children, Rachel, Savannah, and James. Thank you to my friends Bob and Jim, who have helped me through many episodes. Thank you to Ernest Hemingway for his inspiration throughout my life.

Introduction

My name is James Heaton, and I have Bipolar Disorder. Much like the 5.7 million people in the United States who suffer from Bipolar Disorder I have a story to tell. I have shared my stories over the years with family and friends and the common thought is that I have lived many lives in my 47 years. I have been on adventure after adventure, from down low to up high, I've experienced things that most people could only dream of. I wanted to write a book that could help people who have just been diagnosed to understand what is ahead of them. Some people are diagnosed later in life as its difficult to diagnose Bipolar in young people because Bipolar Disorder mimics puberty. Although I was diagnosed at 24, I know for certain that Bipolar was present in my childhood.

Bipolar destroys families and causes divorce and suicide in millions of people yearly. Although there are many medications and procedures to ease the effects of Bipolar there is no cure. Bipolar was originally called Manic Depression and over the years it has been classified into four categories; Bipolar I Disorder, Bipolar II Disorder, Cyclothymic Disorder and Mixed Features.

Bipolar can be treated with several medications as well as Electro Convulsive Therapy (aka ECT or Shock Therapy) and Transcranial Magnetic Stimulation (used in Major Depressive Disorder but not with Bipolar alone). Treatment can also come from stays in mental health facilities and counseling. Most people who suffer from Bipolar have used a combination of treatments and see useful results.

One of the hardest parts of Bipolar is dealing with family and friends. Since Bipolar is an invisible illness most family members see nothing physically wrong with the person and write off the actions as a person unable to control themselves. Periods of depression, uncontrollable crying, severe manic episodes, hypersexuality, uncontrolled spending and other wild actions push family and friends away.

Like many other people who suffer from Bipolar I have watched how it affects my children as I have passed Bipolar to them genetically. I have witnessed firsthand as my daughter fights this horrible disorder daily. But with knowledge comes power, power to understand and cope with the beast. I hope that these stories of my life dealing with Bipolar Disorder can help others find peace.

Bipolar is a destructive force and at times a person with Bipolar can and will make horrible decisions that not only destroy families but can cause legal trouble. Many of my life choices I am ashamed for making and, as embarrassing as those choices are, I have decided to document my life of 47 years. I do this to help others who might be suffering from Bipolar Disorder, people who are just finding out that they have this horrible illness as well as family members who want to be closer to their loved ones during their trials and tribulations.

I've destroyed many friendships, burnt many bridges over the years and done things that have put my life in jeopardy. I'm not proud of those things but hopefully through this book someone can find the help they need. Tips on successfully coping with Bipolar shouldn't be a secret, and along with this book there are many different sources of help available for you today. There are support groups and online communities that are available today that weren't around when I was diagnosed. Basically, this book is what I wish someone had told me when I was diagnosed in 1996.

The Early Years

I was born in 1972 To Diane and Coy Heaton. I was a late baby, and too big for my mother to deliver me vaginally, but the doctors had started the procedure and forced me out. I should have been delivered via C-section, but the doctors made the decision to use forceps on my head. I damaged my mother to the point that I went five days without seeing her. She almost died during my birth and was in recovery for those first five days. I missed the one on one, skin-to-skin time and I wasn't breast fed. I've always held that these things may have impacted my development. Whether the forceps might have caused brain damage is unknown.

My earliest memories of Bipolar are from the mid-1970s when I was in kindergarten. Mostly what I remember is black outs or loss of memory. I remember acting out in a hyperactive fashion that came from manic episodes. I spent a good bit of time in the corner in kindergarten. I simply remember being out of control and unable to calm down.

Many memories from kindergarten are of the teacher spanking me after I did something wrong, but my memory goes from the moments before the act to the moment she spanked me. I have no recollection of what I did wrong. I remember standing in the corner, but no clue as to what I did. This would have been at the age of 5, and this is my earliest memory of being Bipolar. I remember being very hyper and having too much energy. This would have been 1977, and at this time there was no treatment for Bipolar in children.

In the late 1960s, the American Psychiatric Association (APA) formally recognized ADHD as a mental disorder. (3) So, if I had been taken to a psychiatrist, they probably would have diagnosed me as ADHD. This tends to be a common problem with Bipolar misdiagnosis, because the trials of puberty can be so close to the symptoms of Bipolar Disorder.

One instance found me playing kick ball and waiting my turn to kick the ball. The boy behind me was annoying me. One moment I was standing in line and then, in the blink of an eye I was beating the boy with every ounce of energy I had. A teacher pulled me off him and as I stood there looking at his bloody face, I couldn't remember losing it. I spent the rest of the afternoon in the corner for fighting but I was left perplexed at how I went from standing in line to beating somebody up. I suffered a loss of time, something that has happened many times over the years.

Moving through the years I remember being extremely emotional. When I liked a girl, it was so powerful that any rejection felt like death. Every emotion was fully exaggerated and played out. My parents had no idea that their son was suffering from Bipolar. Medication wasn't readily available to treat children so the only treatment I received was stern discipling at the hand of my father.

When you suffer these feelings its all you know. You don't have a comparison to say that your feelings aren't normal. You basically have no idea what normal is. I didn't know to tell my parents anything was wrong because it was all I had ever felt. I suffered with my emotions, feeling like I was going to die every time something happened that pushed me over the edge.

The one thing that stayed constant through out my life was a voice in my head. I recall it as early as my elementary years. It was as if I had a close friend in my head that talked to me, thoughts that were more like a conversation. It was there suggesting things I normally wouldn't have done, almost like the bad side of me. But we discussed things daily, sometimes I caught myself talking out loud to the voice.

I grew up an only child and had two sets of grand parents to spoil me and give me everything I wanted. I obsessed over the typical childhood things; Star Wars, GI Joe, riding bicycles and playing with my friends. I was always the emotional one and try as I might I could never control it. I sought happiness from material things; toys, skateboards and bicycles. I had to have the newest of everything or else I would cry uncontrollably. But even after getting what I wanted, the momentary high of having something new went away and I needed more.

As a child it was apparent that I was gifted with artistic ability. I drew constantly and took private art lessons. I came from an artistically endowed family and was encouraged by my family to pursue my talents. It was an escape for my brain, and when I drew, I went to a quite place that allowed my emotions to flow and create. My parents and grandparents held me to such a high standard of excellence.

I acted out at home, but most times I had no idea what I was doing was wrong. I either blacked out or stubbornly repeated an action over and over. It seemed that whenever something didn't go my way it was the end of my world. I cried or got mad and acted out. This never went over well with my father.

My father came from a long family history of spanking children for discipline sake. He had very little patience for my acting out and spanked me frequently. As I grew older it became worse, he would lose his temper and hit too hard. Using his belt, I often had marks and bruises that I didn't talk about. As I grew older my temper also grew and I developed quite the mouth. I fought back and this became a problem with my father. He didn't see me as a child needing discipline, he saw me as a threat against his masculinity and became more aggressive. Neither of my parents understood me, as they often asked me, "what's wrong with you?"

The aggression from my father damaged me in more ways than just bruises and marks. It unhinged my relationship with men in general. I was untrusting of men and apart from my grandfather I avoided men altogether. I lost years with my father because of his anger and aggression and it wasn't until I was in my 30's that I forgave him. It took years of counselling and deep thought before I could let go of what he did to me.

Having an aggressive father pushed me to be closer to my mother. She protected me from his anger many times and seemed to understand me better. Again, not having a comparison for normal made things very difficult. I had no idea that I was doing anything wrong.

I was very close to my maternal grandfather. My Nanny and Papa were very important to me. I felt that my Papa was more of a father to me than my own father -- they understood me. They also pampered me and gave me everything I wanted. I never felt the pressure of life around them. Their home was open and inviting and a safe place for me. My Nanny practically raised me while my parents worked. At my parents' house I felt tension and insecurity, but with my grandparents I felt safe. This was the first safe place I ever knew.

I had several medical problems as a child, in the fourth grade I had to be hospitalized for exploratory surgery on my stomach. The doctors found a rupturing appendix and ulcers. I had been sick for months before this, missing school daily. It was a very difficult time for me as I was very depressed and in pain.

Sickness and depression went hand in hand with each other. I suffered anxiety when the stomach pain was unbearable and depression from laying on the couch away from my school friends. I missed a lot of school that year forcing me to have a private tutor to help me catch up. The television was my best friend at this point, cartoons and old movies helped me make it through the day.

Middle school found my family moving to a new home, with a new set of friends. It was a chance for a fresh start. The old me didn't exist anymore; he had no direction. The new me was different than everyone around me. My desire to be an individual was very strong and I did everything to be different. This came from me not fitting in, I always felt like I was a loner.

I was obsessed with surfing and skateboarding. I spent my day building ramps to skate on. I was the child without fear. I always took things to extremes, to prove I wasn't afraid of anything. Jumping bicycles or skateboards from on high or running through the woods at night, I did whatever I could to prove that I was indestructible.

I was living in a new neighborhood with new friends and girls all around. Another obsession of mine was the opposite sex. I had been interested in girls from as early as I could remember. I developed deep crushes and if my feelings weren't shared, I became depressed. I had a deep-seated passion toward the opposite sex, I fell easily in love so many times. As with everything else I felt deeper, loved harder, and hurt more than everyone else.

My best friend in middle school was a fellow surfer and skater named Trent who lived down the street. We spent every second with each other and he had a way of getting me in trouble. My parents called him a bad influence, but I adored him.

We spent every second challenging gravity and pushing our luck with skateboard tricks. We rode the biggest ramps, always coming home with bloody knees and scrapes on our bodies. I craved the feeling of almost dying. I was an adrenaline junkie and it got me into a lot of trouble.

Trent also introduced me to sex with girls. He would frequently stop at neighborhood girls houses and sneak off to their bedrooms while I sat and watched cartoons. I was jealous and felt left out. I couldn't understand why he was the desire of so many girls and I was just seen as the cute friend. I was particularly fond of a girl in the neighborhood next to ours. She was always lingering on my mind.

After graduating seventh grade I had a full summer to explore this new world of females. I flirted with my neighborhood crush as often as I could. The Bipolar disorder turned the regular hormones into super hormones. I fantasized about her every minute of every day.

One day I made my move and we came back to my house and we both lost our virginity that day. Even though it was awkward, it was very special. She and I remained friends after the passion had left our relationship. Childhood romances don't last long. And as with any summer love, we moved on from each other.

I've never known what its like to be normal, so I can't really say how much Bipolar increased the puberty experience. All I know is that my sexual desires were painful and flooded my brain. By the time I entered ninth grade I had already slept with three girls. I didn't consider this to be abnormal, everyone lied when it came to sex. Guys said they slept with dozens of girls and girls denied it. There was no way to tell who was lying and who wasn't.

High school was the hardest time for me. The Bipolar was very real, although I had not seen a psychiatrist to confirm anything was wrong with me. I thought everybody felt the way I did. The ups and downs were more frequent and painful. Trying to fit in at school was difficult, I felt awkward and strange. For the most part I was either in fast forward mode or in a dissociative state where I was outside of my body watching from above.

Going into high school I knew who I was. I was the surfer, skater who drew very well and played guitar. I surrounded myself with activities and created an identity. But deep inside I really had no clue who I was. One minute I was listening to metal music and the next I was listening to sappy love songs and getting emotional. I was up and down daily. I went from bouncing off the wall with energy to sitting in my room in silence drawing pictures of beautiful women. There was never an in between, I was always exhausted.

Going into my tenth-grade year I met a young girl named Allison who I cared very deeply for. I was very involved in my church youth group and found a calling with religion. Using prayer and devotionals I had hope to control my ups and downs. I would pray to God to help me act right. I truly believed that a God could help me be normal like everybody else. Allison was drawn to my devotion and knowledge of the bible.

Allison and I dated for over a year and became very close. Although we never had sex I wanted to. But I believed God wanted us to wait for our wedding day. I was obsessed with my future with her, hated our time apart and became very clingy. She saw me as I really was, emotional. She had a firsthand look at my fights with my father. Nobody saw me the way she did. But I could only imagine how it frightened her.

My junior summer I was accepted into the South Carolina Governors School for the Arts. It was a summer program that was held at Furman University. It was an honor to be accepted into the program and I worked very hard to get into it.

Governors School was the first time I had been away from home in a mock college setting. Students lived in dorms for two months and went to class daily. Projects and assignments kept us busy at night and during the day. Governors School was a chance to experience freedom from my parents.

 I made several friends during this time and for the most part I was able to act normal. I was always shy at first and then opened up more and more as time went by. I really had no filter and over time I exposed too much of the real me, it often scared people off. The summer flew by and I graduated from Governors School and received my diploma from the Governor himself. I don't think my family had ever been prouder of me. It was a great sense of accomplishment. I made new friends and tried to keep up with them.

 Allison and I had drifted apart and although we were still dating, I had already cheated on her with a girl from a church trip. Going almost two years with no sexual contact was difficult and the first chance I had I leapt on it. It was a short affair, the first of many times I would cheat on my love interest. Allison and I broke up that summer. She was headed to college and I still had another year of high school.

This was the first big depression I had encountered. I closed myself off after Governors School and slept all day. I was spending my days sitting in my room staring out a window. I was convinced that I wanted to die, so I told my mother that I wanted to kill myself. It was difficult to open up about my feelings of death. She called my grandfather and he convinced her to send me to a psychologist.

I had never been this low before, where I envisioned slicing my wrist or hanging myself. I was so low in a hole that I just wanted to die. Life had no more meaning, I cried myself to sleep nightly. My days were long and full of pain. I was full of anger at everyone. The pain was unimaginable and everyday felt like the end.

The psychologist asked me the standard questions. Did I really want to die? How was my childhood? And in the end, she convinced me that I really didn't want to die, that it was merely a stage I was going through. I can only imagine how different my life would have been if she had pressed harder and discovered I was Bipolar.

I had become withdrawn from the neighborhood kids and they taunted me. On one occasion they threw tennis balls at my house while I was home alone. I asked them to stop but they were cruel and made fun of me for being crazy. They saw me as a loser for getting dumped by my girlfriend and they knew I spent everyday inside. There was so much tension between us. We once were best friends but now we were enemies. Trying to deal with the bombardment of tennis balls at my house I lost it and grabbed my fathers' gun. It was another black out. I pulled the gun on them and told them I would kill them if they didn't stop.

This was a bad move on my part. One of the fathers came to my house and spoke with my dad. I had to apologize and listen to their father tell me I needed help. I knew I needed help; I was losing it daily. But my parents turned to God. Prayer was what I needed, I was in counseling with a lady from church and my parents trusted that she could fix me.

Counseling worked in the moment. But outside of that moment things returned to the dark depression that they were. Making an effort to be better daily helped but it was slow acting. I spent the rest of my summer resetting my mood. Working toward being a better version of myself and seeing things without depression was a daily chore.

My senior year was a fresh start with no girlfriend and no friends from the past. I was a loner. But I found a friendship in a very unlikely place. For my senior year I was a part time student at the Fine Arts Center. I drove daily to FAC and stayed for two periods and then drove back to school. I was surrounded by artists and I felt a kinship with them. We were all weird in our own way and It was a place for me to fit in.

I met several girls to satisfy my sexual appetite. I dated three different girls that year from FAC and I had moved on from Allison. I was reminded years later at my daughters FAC graduation that I was one of only three kids to ever get pulled into the FAC principals' office. The director reminded me that I was caught having sex with a girl in the darkroom. It was nice to be remembered for something.

During my time at the high school I got very close to one of my teachers. He was my political science teacher and he played guitar in a band. We developed a friendship after he asked me to design an album cover for his band. We spent time playing guitar together and hanging out at his house. He gave me my first beer and my first joint. Finally, there was something that could take me away from my insanity. Smoking weed relaxed me and made me feel normal. The alcohol mellowed me out and helped me relax. I knew that doing these things with a teacher was wrong, but he made me feel important. I could have real conversations with him and our love for music made us best friends. He hated all the other teachers and he hated his job. He wanted to be in a band full time, and I idolized him. He turned me onto The Rolling Stones and Sting. He opened the door to my love for music and taught me things I could never learn from school. He was the father I had always dreamed of, the father I never had.

Having an adult friend kept me from having close friends my age. They all seemed immature and boring. Being with an adult exposed me to real world issues, like money and relationship problems. I watched him live his life, making his whole life his own and not answering to anyone. The kids at school were all about school spirit, dating, cars and teenage drama. I was busy creating artistic masterpieces and writing songs. I listened to music from the sixties and dressed like an artist. I isolated myself to protect myself.

My parents were strongly against the time I spent with my adult friend. It just drove me farther apart from my parents. I wanted to get as far from them as I could. I was in a dark place, I listened to depressing music, read depressing books and dressed in dark clothing. I had accepted my depression and learned to mold it into my artistic world. I was fixated on the works of Hemingway and Steinbeck. I had started reading Anne Rice books as well and found the idea of death to be beautiful and alluring.

I applied to the Savannah College of Art and Design. I knew I could get a scholarship from Governors School and SCAD was the best school for art. I was accepted into the Savannah College of Art and Design and couldn't wait until the day I left Greenville SC.

Music and books became my other closest friends. I read novel after novel and listened to Jimi Hendrix. I saw life differently because of these things. Hemingway helped me to see life simply and without complication. Hendrix inspired me to love and live free. I surrounded myself with more and more books, learning so much from dead writers and dead musicians.

Later that year my teacher friend was arrested for having sexual relations with some of the cheerleaders and he and I drifted apart. My focus was on Savannah GA. I wanted to get away from home as soon as I could.

I was known for my art in school. I did a comic strip in the school newspaper, illustrated the yearbook, drew logos for the sports teams and sold portraits over the holidays. I had a job doing the artwork for a screen-printing company. It felt nice to have a mission. Art was an escape for me, as was playing guitar. I spent all my time trying to escape from life, trying to feel something.

Being empty inside, feeling dead to the world, caused me to find life in other areas of my life.

That had become my mission, to simply feel something. From sex with various partners to reading to painting or writing a song. I filled up everyday with these little moments of trying to feel something. When I wasn't doing this, I felt dead inside. I was a walking corpse, reanimated by small actions to fill up my day.

I graduated high school in 1990. I worked for the summer at a frame shop and left for fall semester at SCAD in August. It was the end of a chapter for me, I was finally moving on in my life. I wanted to be away from my hometown and my parents.

College Years

I started college in the fall of 1990, in the town of Savannah GA. Savannah is a historic town on the coast of Georgia, five hours from my hometown of Greenville SC. I was privileged to have my own car and was able to come and go as I pleased. Many of the kids at the school only had bicycles to get around. Having a car allowed me to travel to Tybee Island during the week to surf.

Being a freshman, I had no friends at the college but was quick to make friends with my hall mates. My first friend was named Jeff and he was a drummer. We quickly formed a band and practiced weekly. Our band, Yuk Foo, played classic rock and was more of a novelty. Compared to bands I've played with over the years we were very juvenile and needed a great deal of practice. I had two hobbies; surfing and music, and my classes to keep me busy.

I felt older and wiser. I had so much freedom. Nobody was there to tell me to go to bed or complain because my music was too loud. If I wanted to stay up all night drawing nobody could complain. The college was spread all over town and I made my way from building to building. I came and went on my own accord and I felt alive.

It wasn't long before alcohol became another hobby. We spent our Fridays and Saturdays drinking in a town that shuts down on Thursdays and becomes a party town the whole weekend. We went from party to party walking around the city. People would throw keggers in the back yard of the historic homes and drink until the beer ran out. After a while we moved on to liquor, making the most of every weekend.

My manic phases were legendary, and people loved me for my wild antics and crazy stunts. I was always the life of the party. And I always had a different girl every weekend. My Bipolar Disorder was wide open, and my hypersexuality was trailing in a close second. Mix those two with alcohol and I was a ticking time bomb. I was beginning to black out and not remember anything from the night before. I relied on my friends to fill me in on my hijinks and shenanigans. Every Sunday I would swear that this was the last weekend I would drink, and I would spend my time trying to be a better student. That never worked, I always feel off the wagon and started back the following weekend.

I had started to lose control and had a few run ins with the law. On one instance we took a blow-up doll to the top of the building and filled it up with water and ketchup. We then had one of the guys tell the security guard at the door that a girl was going to jump. The guard was doing his best to talk the girl down but after a few minutes we tossed her off the roof. She hit the ground hard and exploded. We all got written-up for that instance. Another night I let a pet rat lose on the security guard and scared him silly. He called his Sergeant and a few police officers to question me. I was heavily intoxicated and got written-up again.

I had to go before a review board and explain myself. Their conclusion was that I had a drinking problem and I was placed on probation over the Christmas Holidays. My parents had no idea, so when I came home from school, they thought everything was fine. Being home was tough with no alcohol or weed to hold me over. I longed to return to school and be back with my friends.

Being back around my parents I felt the old depression surface. They were controlling and treated me life a little child. It was difficult to go from complete freedom to being treated like a toddler. I longed to be back in school. I couldn't get back fast enough.

After the holiday break we had a few new faces on the hall and one of them was able to score drugs for us. I started lightly with just weed and mushrooms. The weed helped me to create beautiful works of art and I looked at it as a positive thing. I was getting good grades and becoming my teacher's favorite student.

Because of Governors School I was able to secure a nice scholarship but SCAD was still expensive. My parents had moved into a smaller house and sold one of their cars to afford my tuition. Looking back at how selfish I was, partying and drinking while my parents suffered to pay my way, I feel ashamed for my actions. If only I was able to have self-control. But that's the thing about Bipolar Disorder, it takes that control away and like a puppet you do what your manic phases command. Alcohol increases that problem and makes it even worse. But I was going easy on the booze, I spent my weekends high and felt more in control.

I was spending more time surfing and enjoyed playing with the dolphins that frequented the island. I isolated myself and only went out one night a week. Along with playing at the bars with my band I had also secured a job at a seafood restaurant. But after a while I craved a deeper high. I was using LSD and smoking weed daily. I cancelled my meal plan and got a cash refund to buy more drugs. I had also discovered Ecstasy and was enjoying having sex with the effects of drugs. I can't count the number of times I woke up beside a stranger the next morning and, on a few occasions, I would leave their home and have no idea where I was. All of this scared me but the addiction to the high was so strong. I really did begin to think I had a problem.

During this time, I developed a relationship with a young Goth student named Sarah. She was dark and beautiful, and she loved to have sex. She was the perfect girlfriend, but I was not the perfect boyfriend. On the nights I would drink, I became aggressive and verbally abusive. The next day I would apologize, and she would forgive me. It was a dark cycle that repeated itself every weekend. But she tolerated it and I couldn't break the habit. She drank heavily too, as did most of the students. I had become bored with alcohol and hallucinogens and wanted something harder.

My hall mate was able to score some heroin and cocaine. I had never tried either and was eager to see what the fuss was about. I shot up one night before going out with Sarah. The stomach pain was incredible but the high was unlike any high I had ever experienced. Needless to say, I don't remember anything from that night and woke up in Sarah's bed the next morning. The next day I was down in a hole and used the coke to pick myself up. It was like a manic phase but stronger. I had so much energy and was able to bypass the hangover from the heroin.

It was getting close to spring break and my drug use was out of control. I was worried about my classes, and I was worried about my father. He had told me he was dealing with a cancer scare and he didn't want me to worry. All the while my parents were struggling to pay for my tuition.

I had stopped using the heroin and coke, as it was a habit I couldn't afford. So, I spent most nights on LSD. It had become common place for me to go night surfing with some of my friends. Not only was it scary but doing it on LSD was amazing. Being out in the dark water surround by the night was an adrenaline rush. Life had become so bland that I was risking my life to feel something. I put my life on the line surfing in shark infested water at night to feel alive. All the while high on LSD. It was at this point I knew I was totally out of control.

I was totally dead inside, desperate to feel something. Acting out, drinking, surfing at night, and doing drugs gave me mere moments of life. I was depressed and filling the void any way, I could. Today we are surrounded by pamphlets, banners, ads and information about depression and depression related medication. Had that been the case in 1990 I think I might have found help earlier.

It was a few weeks after spring break that I got a letter saying I had a meeting with the Dean of Finance about my financial situation. I was very nervous about this and decided to drop acid before going to see her. In my mind I knew this was a bad idea, but I did it anyway.

Her office was nicely decorated in one of the historic buildings that made Savannah the city it was. She wore a nice business suit and was very proper. She invited me in and asked me to sit. She explained that I was behind in my payment plan and that I needed to get caught up or be on suspension until it was paid. She expressed concern over my dad's cancer and told me she knew this was an issue but not an excuse. I was feeling the effects of the LSD but at the same time I felt a stirring of emotion. A rage was building in me, how dare she be so cold and calloused. This was the first eruption in my first real Bipolar break. Everything came to the surface. Like an explosion I stood up and told her to go fuck herself. I pushed things off her desk and told her she was a cold-hearted bitch and that I was out, I quit. She was terrified and appeared to be in shock. My heart was beating so hard and I felt like my face was going to explode. I rushed out of the office and walked back to my dorm room. I collapsed on my bed and cried. My heart was still pounding. It was as if all the manic episodes and the depressive episodes over the years just exploded like a volcano. I was feeling every emotion all at once. It took me hours to call down.

This was the first rage explosion I had ever had that was this intense. I had to use all my self-control to keep from breaking everything in front of me. I was very dangerous at this point, both to myself and to others.

I received a note the next day ordering me to vacate the dorm within 72 hours. I called my parents and told them I wanted to come home. I told them I couldn't take it anymore and I needed to leave. They told me they would be down in two days. I took this as I had two days to party like I had never partied before.

We made our way around town going from apartment to apartment. Wherever the alcohol was, we were there. We wound up in a fancy apartment on the other side of town with people we didn't know. There was a kid selling LSD and PCP and several kegs. I had brought my own bottle of Irish whiskey. It was at this party that we saw this one kid running around with a bath towel around his neck like a cape saying he was superman. He was jumping off everything. His friends said he did 10 hits of acid; we all had a great laugh but then he got on the third story balcony and stood on the railing. And just like that he fell. Girls screamed, guys laughed and then someone said he busted his head. We all left very fast, that kid died that night from a head injury. We ran when we heard the sirens, off to another party.

 Around 3am we got our surfboards and drove to Tybee Island for my last night surf. I sat on my board surrounded by darkness on every side except for the lights in the parking lot. The water was cold, and it was peaceful. I knew I had messed up; I knew I had destroyed everything. A part of me was glad it was over, glad that I was free from the insanity that I had created. What was wrong with me. Why did I have no self-control? It was a moment of clarity. Sitting in the dark surrounded by my thoughts. I knew there was something wrong with me.

We made our way home, stopping for breakfast. This was my last day in hell. A hell I had created. Savannah has a distinct smell from the paper mills. Today was going to be the last day I would smell that. My parents showed up shortly after noon and we loaded up my belongings. I said my goodbyes and left that town. I was very hung over and my dad commented that I reeked of alcohol. He had no idea what I had done, nobody did. It was my cross to bear.

After I arrived home, I made a promise to myself. No more alcohol. Weed was still my friend but no more drinking. I missed surfing and I missed my time with the dolphins. I wanted to be closer to the ocean and start over. I felt like my life as an artist was over, without an education and degree what could I ever hope to accomplish?

A New Life

Being back in Greenville was depressing. I got a job working in a yogurt shop and found a pot connection. Living at home felt like I was going backwards. Back to being treated like a kid, getting yelled at for stupid mistakes. I wasn't seen as a 19-year-old, but more like a 5-year-old. My father and I argued frequently, and I felt like I wasn't wanted in their home. I had nowhere else to go and spent much of my time at my grandparents hanging out. There I was welcome and appreciated.

I was in a discovery phase. Art had gone from being a chance at a good life to an innovation. I was doing caricatures for money at local festivals, but it wasn't a fine art it was more of a novelty. I wanted to do something that mattered. And I needed some form of an adrenaline rush.

I found an ad for 2 for 1 scuba certification in a local magazine. I tore it out and held onto it. I had been working steadily at the yogurt shop and needed a direction in my life. So, I spent my time reading Scuba Diving magazines. I could be close to the ocean and if I tried hard enough, I could be an instructor, So I saved my money and asked my dad to be my partner. We took the introduction course together.

Diving offered the adrenaline rush I needed and the calming atmosphere I missed with surfing. I quit my job at the yogurt shop and went to work at a sporting good shop, learning everything I could about Scuba equipment. Being focused and having a direction helped with the manic episodes, but even at this point I didn't even know what the words Bipolar meant. I had never heard about Manic Depression, except from Jimi Hendrix. I would never have guessed that I was suffering from a mental disease.

I knew that Hemingway had committed suicide because of his depression, but at this point in my life I had no knowledge of Bipolar Disorder. Unlike today, there weren't commercials for medications that openly discussed mental illness on television.

I enrolled in a Dive Master course at the local dive shop and started my training. My grandfather was helping me pay for the courses, he had a plan to retire in Florida and open a dive shop for me to run. I was looking forward to spending my adult years with him. Everything was moving smoothly.

The owner of the dive shop came to the sporting good store to see what her competition was selling. I recognized her, and she recognized me. She told me I could come to work for her and make more money and get my certification to repair equipment. It was a no brainer; things were really going my way.

Linda had owned Adventures in Scuba for years. She had a large shop; half scuba, half exotic fish. She was a short heavy-set lady with beautiful blond hair. She wore bright colors and was always happy. She had the demeanor of a sweet mother figure. She treated me like I was her own son. Over time I told her my story about my alcohol and drug addiction. She offered to help me stay clean. Whenever I felt the urge to drink, I could call her, and she would talk to me for hours until I no longer had the desire. She was like a sponsor without having to do AA. I worked with her for a year while I trained to become a Divemaster. In that time, I developed a friendship with Linda's' son, Shane and his girlfriend Tammy. We became inseparable. Every weekend we were at the lakes with dive classes, loading tanks and helping with tours.

I became obsessed with deep dives. It was an adrenaline rush and I loved the thrill of diving into the deep black water. It was the same with everything I did, I had to take it to the most extreme. One of the effects of deep diving is nitrogen narcosis. Also known as narcing, nitrogen narcosis gives you a high, almost confusing feeling when you dive to depths of 100 feet or more. I loved the natural high that I got from pushing it to the deeper depths.

Back at the dive shop, Linda gave me a lot of responsibilities, one of which was helping at the Scuba club meeting. It was there I met a woman nine years my senior, who I fell in love with. It was love at first site, she was tall and had beautiful dark hair. She wasn't very friendly though. I told Linda that I wanted to get to know her. Linda explained that her name was Deborah and she was also a divemaster. Linda wanted her to come into the shop and learn about the gear, and she wanted me to teach her.

Deb and I became close rather quickly. She was taken with my lust for life, and she had just gotten out of a bad marriage and liked the idea of a younger man. I was 20 and she was 29, this didn't go over very well with my parents. But I didn't care, I was in love. I opened up to Deb about my addictions and my ups and downs. She admired me for fighting my demons.

Deb and I dated for several months, growing closer to each other. I spent the night at her place often, enjoying the escape from home. My Bipolar Disorder seemed to be under control, I wasn't experiencing manic episodes just a steady mood.

I was spending every free moment with Deb. Diving brought us together and we spent every weekend diving together. Being with her made me feel mature and full of life. Just like being close to my high school teacher, I enjoyed the company of someone older than me. Even though I spent my time reading comics, watching cartoons and playing video games I was very mature for my age. I craved mature conversation and time with mature people. Deborah offered me a way to feel mature while being a kid.

It was time for me to travel to Florida to take my instructor course. It was a two-week course with the exam on a Saturday. My grandfather said he had met Deb at the scuba shop and wanted to know if Deb could come down and stay. I was fine with it, she helped me focus, or at least I thought she did.

When my grandfather and Deb arrived, I found it almost impossible to focus on my studies. The class was divided into half classroom and half water training. I dove every day, sometimes in the pools and other times in the ocean. At night I went out with Deb instead of studying.

The Bipolar was creeping up on me, this time in the form of bad decisions. Out of the blue I got it in my head that I wanted to propose to Deb on the beach. I should have been focusing on my studies but instead I was like a schoolboy fawning over his new love. My grandfather loaned me the money for a ring, and I waited until that night to propose to Deb.

We walked out to a secluded stretch of the beach and I got down on one knee and proposed. She quickly said yes, and just like that I made a decision that would change the rest of my life.

The test was that Saturday and I knew I was ill prepared. I struggled through the formulas and missed more questions than was allowed. In a matter of days, I had wasted my time, my money and blew my future. I could come back and take the test a month from the date for a nominal fee of course. I had let my grandfather down; he was disappointed in me and told me that having Deb there was a mistake.

When Deb and I arrived home, she moved in with me so that we could save for the wedding. It was one night after we got home from Florida that I got a call at 2am. Nothing good ever comes from a call at 2am. It was Linda, she had died in a dive accident at night. She had drowned during a night dive on a reef in Florida. I was crushed. Linda had become like a mother to me, she was the reason I was able to refrain from drinking, she was the reason I had made it this far.

Losing Linda was a crushing blow. I felt an emptiness inside. I cried for several days whenever I thought about her being gone. I felt like my love for diving had slipped right past me and I was without a future.

Linda was buried three days later, and then I quit the dive shop. I was through with diving. I needed to move on from this life. My grandfather was very disappointed, but he understood. This was a traumatic event.

Married with Children

Bipolar effects decision making. It makes the rational decisions less attractive and pushes you to go to the extremes. The wildest thing you can think of seems normal and like a good decision. After a while it feels like you only make bad decisions and if forces you to question everything.

Deb and I were married December 5th, 1992. In a few short years I had dropped out of college, dropped out of diving and became a young husband. I was still the immature kid who loved cartoons, video games, comic books and skateboarding. But now I had a 29-year-old wife who had a bright future at Michelin in the graphic arts department. We moved into our first apartment and now I was trying to decide how to make a living.

I decided to go back to my art. I picked up doing caricatures at parties and events. My grandfather felt this had big money-making potential if we expanded. We set out on the local festival circuit, and then the holiday fair circuit. We spent the entire year traveling from event to event. I added airbrushing to the mix and immediately we were making good money. My grandfather decided to add screen printing to the mix, and we made even more money.

Moreover, Deb was pregnant. I had so much pressure on me to run a company, to be a family man and now I was going to be a father. My Bipolar Disorder had been dormant for quite some time. My moods had remained even with little to no manic moods. It was almost like it was just waiting to come out at the worst time possible.

My grandfather and I were busy running a screen-printing shop and I was doing airbrushing on t-shirts and motorcycles. Business was good for a time, but it started dropping. There was quite the competition in the local market.

On December 12th, 1993 Rachel Arielle Heaton was born. I was 21 yrs. old and just a kid. She came into our lives like a rocket, and my life would never be the same. I don't know if it was the Bipolar Disorder, but I loved that little girl more than I had ever loved anything. She was the soul focus in my life, I lived everyday for her. It was hard to believe I was a father; it was the greatest feeling I had ever had.

Being a father was a big responsibility and I tried as hard as anyone. Mentally I wasn't capable of being both a husband and a father. I put all my focus on

Rachel and worked on being the worlds greatest father. This was difficult for Deb as she never really developed a relationship with Rachel.

As 1994 came I watched my business crumble. We couldn't give the pricing other screen printers offered and the bills were too much to cope with. We sold our screen-printing shop to a couple from NC and took a loss. My dream of being in business with my grandfather was short lived and I was sad to see it end.

I had an interest in law enforcement from a young age. Mostly my fixation of Magnum P.I. on television as a child. Growing up I idolized Batman as the greatest crime fighter and wanted to be just like him. That stuck with me through out the years. The idea of being morally superior to others struck a chord with me. Laws were meant to be followed, and someone needed to be there to enforce them. I had given up on art and scuba diving, it was time for something new in my life.

 I thought that being a policeman would give me some respect, so I filled out applications and decided to get my foot in the door. I was told to start in security and go from there. I went to work for the mall security for six months and then got hired by the Greenville Detention Center. It was a big step for me, it was a real job and it came with good pay and benefits. This was a positive change for my family. I spent a year working at the Detention Center, went to the police academy and graduated. I was the smallest guy in my graduating class, standing 5'11" and weighting 120 lbs. I tried to bulk up, but it just wasn't happening. It was difficult to be an intimidating guard around inmates twice my size.

My manic phases had manifested into rage. I got angry very easy and took it out on the inmates. There were simple rules that needed to be followed but most of the guards overlooked things. I was of the mindset that all rules needed to be followed without exception. I started getting written up for being overly aggressive towards the inmates.

We had to be physical with inmates through out the day. Fights were common, getting hit was a daily act. I took down guys twice my size. My anger would push me over the edge, and I could handle the biggest guy. I was always the first to volunteer when things got rough.

I had no military background and most of the other guards had ten years on me. I really wanted to work for the Sheriffs office but every time I applied; I was turned down because of lack of experience.

After a year working with the Detention center, I was dismissed for being overly aggressive to the inmates. I took advantage of the retirement I had started and used it to get my Private Detectives license. I trained for 6 months with a local detective and then applied for my own agency license.

In my mind I believed I could be just like Magnum P.I., a relaxed investigator with his own office and steady cliental. Before I could get to that level, I needed to make a name for myself. I needed time to build up a client base. I took a job as a store detective to help with finances until my business picked up.

Working at the Detention Center was difficult in many ways but being stuck in a sealed building with germs and viruses I developed several obsessive compulsions. I wore rubber gloves when I needed to deal with the trash or clean. I became obsessed with washing my hands, going as far to buy a fresh bar of soap for every time I washed my hands. It wasn't uncommon for me to have 30 – 40 bars of soap in my bathroom. I was overly organized with my clothes, folding and organizing according to colors. I was obsessed with order, aligning things through out the house.

I had developed Obsessive Compulsive Disorder. Order and cleanliness made me feel safe. I obsessed over what germs could do, how they could be covering every surface. I feared for my child's safety. I went as far as doing things in three's, locking the door three times, flipping the light switch three times. It had taken over my life and I hated it.

After a year of working at the department store with a young lady named Wendy, we developed quite the friendship, More like brother and sister. We spent 8 hours a day locked up in a video surveillance room watching shoplifters. She had mentioned how she thought I was Bipolar and that I exhibited signs of OCD. I blew it off and laughed. I really had no clue what any of that meant. But I knew that my disorders were affecting my life.

Deb and I found out that she was pregnant with our second child at the first of the year. I was excited to say the least, but weary of being able to handle two kids. Rachel was quite the handful.

It was around that time that I was injured while arresting a shoplifter. I had my right shoulder pulled behind my back, causing a tear in my pectoral muscle and damage to the shoulder. I was laid up at home when Wendy was let go because of budget cuts. I felt useless all the time. I was unable to do basic things that required two arms and I just became increasingly frustrated.

A few weeks later the store closed costing me my job. It was just three weeks before my surgery. I had the surgery just a week after Deb gave birth to Savannah Eryn Heaton on July 4th, 1997. The surgery cost me the use of my right arm for 3 months. There was daily physical therapy combined with a new baby.

I was able to hire Wendy as a detective because business was picking up. We mostly did divorce cases and served process paperwork. I was running the office out of my home until I could find a cheap office to rent.

Shortly after Savannah was born, I went to a psychiatrist. It was a big step for me, but the OCD had gotten out of hand and my manic phases were more aggressive. Going to a doctor meant facing the fact something was wrong with me. It was a life changing decision.

The doctor was an older male who seemed quite wealthy. He was dressed in very nice clothes, wore an expensive watch and the office was very fancy with lots of expensive art. The lobby was cold and silent. There were other people waiting like me, I wondered what brought them to this place. Were they broken like me? The doctor called me back to his office and he talked with me for about 15 minutes then sent me into a room to answer about 100 questions of a written test. It was all multiple questions and made every effort to answer them correctly. After I answered the questionnaire, he had me wait another 15 minutes in the lobby, then called me back into his office.

He told me that he was diagnosing me with Bipolar disorder, and OCD. He prescribed some drugs and handed me a few brochures. He told me it would be helpful to see a counselor but not required,

It was 1997 -- Google wasn't a thing. I only had medical books at the library to give me a clue as to what Bipolar disorder was. They were no help, I learned nothing from them. They all basically said periods of manic phases mixed with bouts of depression. There were no special diets, nothing that told how this happened, no books or anything to explain to me what all this meant to my life.

The meds made me sleepy, gave me dry mouth and caused erectile dysfunction. I stayed on them for a month and then gave up on them.

Meanwhile my business was booming. I had the largest agency in the area and now had 2 employees working full time with me. The money was coming in and I was spending it as fast as I could make it. I lavished my daughters with gifts every time I took on a new case. I was having a hard time keeping it under control. All the while I had the words Bipolar Disorder stuck in the back of my head. I was now a label. I was a medical diagnosis. And as hard as I tried, I still couldn't find a single book to help me with my diagnosis. Most everything was medical jargon that did nothing but confuse me. I had to accept the fact that I was different now, I was Bipolar.

The Big Break

Over the next few years I had pulled away from wife. There were temptations at every turn. I saw her as a mother and no longer as the hot wife I once had. I wanted to love her the same, but I couldn't see her as the same woman when we first met. I had been sleeping with a secretary from a firm that I worked with. It wasn't a serious relationship, more of a fling when it was convenient. It was a heavy guilt but not enough for me to come clean and tell my wife.

Deb and I fought more and more, and I had written notes telling her I wanted to leave. She always talked me into staying for the kids. But I never felt like I was part of things. I had been seeing a new psychiatrist because my previous doctor's wife hired me to investigate him. The money was too good to turn down, so I just changed to another doctor in the practice.

I had been on Zoloft and Prozac off and on for a year or so. I countered the effects with naps and Viagra. In the fall of 2000 Deb and I found out she was again pregnant. This came as a surprise because I thought she was on birth control. I've always suspected it was away to keep me to stay in the family.

James Patrick Heaton was born May 7th, 2001. He was a beautiful baby boy and his sisters loved him. I was overjoyed with his birth and the manic phases rolled right in. But this was the beginning of the end.

A few weeks after James birth I met a new client named Tonja. She came into my office pregnant and carrying a little boy. She has red curly hair, stood 5' tall and had peanut butter smeared on her top. She told me that her husband was cheating on her.

As we began to talk, she told me of her husband, how he owned a cleaning service and used it to have sex with various women. I realized I knew her husband from years ago in the church group I belonged to. I had never liked him and was happy to bust him cheating. She was without any money and had found an attorney to work pro bono for her. I offered to do the same. I was intoxicated by her and would have done anything for her. The Bipolar had turned a simple attraction into the greatest love the world had ever seen.

Tonja and I talked daily about her case and with each conversation the temptation grew stronger. I knew I had strong feelings for her. I regretted staying with Deb, because if I was free, I could be with Tonja.

I worked her case for three weeks and got all the evidence I needed that her husband was in fact cheating. I was even able to search his computers hard drive and copy numerous nudes he regularly sent out to girls on chat groups. We had an airtight solid case and her attorney was thrilled. After her preliminary hearing she and I met for dinner at Olive Garden. After dinner we sat out in my car and talked for over an hour. I could have listened to her for hours. It was there that we kissed and then decided to go get a hotel room. I had no reserve, no guilt, nothing but adrenaline at the thought of making love to her.

I had stopped caring about getting caught, I was spending all my free time with her. Rarely going home. But so much of that time is a blur. I do remember my birthday in July having a get together with family and then leaving and going to a hotel room with Tonja. She and I talked about the future and she was as open to being together with me as I was her.

Finally, one day in August I had enough and told Deb that I was seeing someone else. She broke down and cried, I tried to say something that would mean something. I realized what I had done, I was aware that I had just ended my marriage. I had just lost my children. For a period after this Deb wanted me back, she wanted me to end things with Tonja and come back home. And I tried. I gave an honest attempt, but I had strong feelings for Tonja.

My family hated me. They were furious and I was isolated and alone. I had been living out of my office for weeks until I found a condominium for rent. I felt like any minute more I would break. To make things worse I had secured an attorney to handle the case only to have Deb come in and take him from me. He was a friend, but she had more money than I did, and I was all alone and relying on my income to support me. The problem was I was barely working. I was staying drunk all the time and blowing cases left and right. The State Law Enforcement Agency had me under investigation for taking clients money and not working their cases. I had been given a month to straighten out the problems, but my head wasn't in it.

September 11th, 2001, I accepted service from my wife's attorney at their office. I then went to my office to curl up with coffee and whiskey. One of the other tenants from downstairs came up and asked if I was watching the television. I turned it on to see the madness. I was terrified at what I saw. The world was crashing down around me and none of my family was speaking to me, the only person I had was Tonja. I was worried about my children, but the schools had been told not to talk to me or acknowledge me as a parental figure. I wasn't allowed in the schools to see my kids.

After our preliminary hearing child support was set at an unreasonable amount, I struggled to pay it and keep my office open. It was then that I decided to retire. I could no longer keep handling cases and deal with the insanity of my personal life. I was able to get a job at Radio Shack.

I had a small Bipolar break one night when Deb refused to let me see my kids. I lost my cool and started threatening to take my kids and run far away. I could hear Rachel in the background screaming to talk to me. So, I took what pills I had and chased it with whiskey. Tonja and my mother told me to go to the hospital and after I started losing consciousness I decided to drive to the hospital and check myself in. But Deb had found out and several police officers were waiting for me. They roughed me up and handcuffed me to a bed and checked me in. After they pumped my stomach, they released me saying I wasn't being charged. As soon as I was able to stand, I got up and walked out. It took me an hour to get to my condo where I found a note from the police saying they had searched my apartment and took all my firearms for my safety. I later found out that my father had let them into my apartment and told them I was going crazy and was going to hurt myself.

In January of 2002 I found out that Debs attorney had convinced my parents to agree to testify in court that I was unfit as a parent and that I needed supervised custody. I was crushed. I was betrayed and my mind was racing. I was angry, hurt and losing grip on reality.

Here it was. The big break. My world was over, and Deb had just ended it. I rushed out of the attorney's office and got into my mothers' car. I drove home as fast as I could, on the phone yelling at my mother for betraying me. I told her I was going to end it and she could live with the guilt of betraying me. I pulled the car in the driveway sliding on the ice, almost hitting the house. I went inside and grabbed every bottle of pills I could find, being picky and going for sleeping pills, pain pills and muscle relaxers. I chased them down with a bottle of whiskey and then put my gun in my mouth. I remember crying and thinking of my kids. The pain was so intense, I wanted to die at that moment. I just needed to get numb enough to pull the trigger. I was terrified but this was it, how could I come back from this. Things got blurry, I started losing consciousness.

I remember my father kicking in my door and grabbing my gun. He was screaming my name and looking through the pill bottles. He knew it was bad. I was barely breathing, and he was holding me as he waited for the ambulance.

I died in the ambulance for two minutes and thirty seconds. The paramedics were able to revive me and get me to the hospital. At the hospital they were able to pump my stomach and force feed me charcoal paste. I was very out of it for several hours.

As soon as I was able to stay awake, they transported me to the psychiatric hospital that was adjoined with the hospital. I wasn't allowed any personal items and was only given a t-shirt and a pair of sweatpants. I attended classes during the day, and group therapy. I felt like everyone there was crazy. I wasn't crazy I was just depressed. I spent a week begging to be released. I held strong to the notion that I wasn't crazy I just didn't want to live. There it was. Full circle from age 16, when I first felt the urge to die to now at age 29 sitting in a mental hospital wanting to end it all. This was my big Bipolar break. I went from having a happy family to being in a mental hospital, at the end of a nasty divorce with three kids I wasn't allowed to see. I had completely lost grip of all that was stable in my life. I needed help.

In all honesty I should have spent more than a week in the hospital, but my job was at stake. Not to mention child support had to be paid. The courts were less than understanding about any circumstance that prevented you from paying what you owed. It would be years before I stepped foot back into a mental hospital, but it was there to help me, and I should have been back sooner.

I was living with my parents at this point and my relationship with Tonja had survived almost a year, but it was coming to an end. After I left the hospital, I had my divorce hearing to look forward to. I admitted to cheating on my wife and was given visitation of my children. This in itself was painful. It was a cut on my ability to be a functioning parent. I raised Rachel and Savannah and never really had a chance with James. They were my children; I should have been given joint custody, but Deb couldn't see past the adultery. I wanted to forget it and move on, but it was way too soon. Time would heal all wounds, but my head was full of clutter.

Shortly after the divorce I had the kids for the weekend, and we went to a fast food restaurant. Tonja was with us and she had her kids, we were doing the best to make a family time out of things. James was with me at the register and the lady at the counter asked if he had water on the brain. I was instantly offended and asked what she meant. She told me her grandchild had suffered from that and James looked like him. I guess I had never really noticed but his head was larger than normal. This sat with me, I needed some answers. I took him to the doctor and was sent in for scans. Deb thought I was reacting foolishly and that he was fine. The CAT Scans showed a tumor in between the brains hemispheres, and we were told it needed to be removed immediately.

I was in full panic mode; my son had a tumor in his brain, and I was helpless to help him. And here I was in the hospital with a woman who hated me. She tried to exclude me in everything, but I pushed back and made myself a part of every conversation with the doctor. His first surgery to remove the tumor was partially successful, but it was going to take several more surgeries to remove the entire tumor.

James spent several weeks in the hospital and the war between his mother and me waged heavy. She had me removed from his bed side by security because it wasn't my scheduled visitation date. I wasn't allowed to be near him unless it was a surgery and the doctors were told they couldn't talk to me. So much was happening, and I was miles away from where I needed to be. Self-doubt engulfed me and I wanted to be as far away as I could.

I was torn between wanting to stay and fight; and flee to a place far, far away. I knew the right thing to do was stay and be with my children, but I feared what I might do.

I decided to flee the situation and drove to Key West, Florida for a few days. My intentions were to stay. I had decided the kids didn't need me. What use was I to them? How could I be a real father if I wasn't even allowed to be beside them when they needed me the most? The noise in my head was so loud, the voice just kept saying to get away. Part of me knew that my place was beside my son and needed to go home, but the voice kept telling me that I needed to just keep running.

After three days I drove home, only to be told I had to wait until my scheduled visitation to see James. I had lost my job at Radio Shack because I took off time to be with my son in the hospital. So now I was behind in child support. And I was being called into court to answer for it.

The judge had no sympathy for my situation and ordered me incarcerated until I could get my balance caught up. I was placed in isolation because I was a former employee of the detention center. Over the next few months this happened four more times. Each time my grandfather bailed me out. I spent a day at most each time in the jail, but it felt like a lifetime.

The short cord that I was dangling on kept getting shorter. I was at wits end and I just wanted to get far away from Deborah. She was completely uninterested in my struggle and didn't care that I couldn't make enough to pay child support on the jobs that I could get. James was able to come home and was starting chemotherapy for the cancer. I was still only allowed to see the kids every other weekend.

This was the beginning of Rachels trauma. She missed me very much and had started acting out. She was seeing the school counselor for her depression. She and I had been inseparable before the divorce and now we hardly saw each other. This was all my fault; this was all on my hands. That guilt weighted on me heavily, eating at me daily.

I was working at a hotel as the night auditor during this time. It was close to my parents' home where I was living. I was able to make extra money by writing reports for some friends I made at the local police department. I spent a few months saving money by living with my parents. Every dime went to child support and my savings. I needed to get far away from this insanity.

I found out that I could transfer my position anywhere in the country if I did it on the hotel computer. I needed to distance myself from the insanity because it was destroying me. I didn't want to leave my kids but what use was I to them? I was depressed and angry at the situation. I hated their mother and fought with her constantly. There was no resolve to this madness; I could try and raise the money to go back to court for a better custodial situation, but I was barely able to pay child support.

So, I put in for the night auditor position at the Savannah, Georgia location. I packed up all my belongings and told my daughters goodbye. They were crushed at losing me, but I was not able to stay. I needed to heal, and I couldn't do it so close to their mother. I needed my space. My parents weren't happy, but they understood. Somehow, I had convinced myself this was for the best, all the while my daughters cried as I left them.

Far from Home

Savannah was everything I needed. It was a different world, a place for me to recover. I had a small apartment and a bicycle to get around. I was working 12-hour shifts at the hotel and saving all my money for rent, food and child support. On my nights off I spent my time at The Rail, a small Irish bar in the historic district. I made friends with the bartender; an old Irishman named Mike. I drank my fill at night and then made my way home on my bicycle.

Music had always played a part in my life. I had my guitar and played it daily. But I needed music to make it through the day. In my youth I was obsessed with Jimi Hendrix, Sting, The Rolling Stones and Eric Clapton. Music was always there for me to negate my mood. I could bring myself up or down with a song. In Savannah I had three artists that I listened to; Norah Jones, Life House, and The Counting Crows. On the bus or on my bike I always had my cd player in my backpack, listening to my favorite songs. They kept me alive when I was suicidal, they brought me down with the manic phases. And the suicidal thoughts were heavy. I spent my days off passed out on sleeping pills and rum. I was drinking more and more to self-medicate. I had no doctor to speak of, money was scarce, and times were getting tougher.

My electricity had been turned off and my water was on the verge of being turned off. I was behind in child support, but my grandfather was helping as much as he could. I had obviously made a mistake by moving away from living with my parents where my expenses were covered. Paying rent and other expenses wasn't working. And the voices were getting louder. I had tried to overdose on several occasions but fell short each time because I just couldn't leave Rachel and Savannah. I missed my daughters so much. They were able to visit with my parents a few times, but it only made the pain worse when they left.

I was dead inside, what exactly was I living for? A weekend visit with my children once a month? Memories of being a good father? What was keeping me alive? I couldn't see a rainbow on the edge of this, all I could feel was severe depression. Tonja and I had been over for a while and I only had the occasional fling with girls I met at the hotel or the bar. It was all meaningless and without real feelings.

I had to use a pay phone to call my daughters, I had no cell phone. I called them at work sometime but mostly in the evening from the convenience store pay phone down the street. One night I called, and Deb told me that Rachel had homework and couldn't speak to me. This infuriated me, the rules stated I was allowed to talk to them daily. But she refused to let me talk to them. This pushed me over the edge, I was already close to breaking. That night on the way to work I stopped and picked up a six pack of beer. I was all alone at the hotel at night, so nobody was there to stop me form drinking. I finished off the six pack and with the courage that came from a six pack of beer I sat down to pen an email to Deb.

I told her that I had a large collection of images from the days when we were married. Images that were very embarrassing if they were put on a web site. I threatened to create a web site and charge users to get in and use the money to hire an attorney to get custody of the kids if she didn't give me more time with them. Bipolar and alcohol are a dangerous mixture and I was at the edge of insanity. I didn't care for the repercussions of my actions; I just wanted my kids and I didn't care how I got them.

The next day I instantly regretted sending that email. I had been very drunk and on an emotional roller coaster. It took a week before one of Savannahs Police officers came to my door. I didn't answer but they left a card on my door. My mother was able to talk to a police friend and find out I was being charged with blackmail and failure to pay child support. I had two warrants out for my arrest. I had really messed up and my only option was to run.

My parents came down with the girls and we talked. I had sold almost all my belongings and had enough money to live in the Bahamas until I could get a job. The plan was for my dad to drive me to Fort Lauderdale and I catch a plane to Nassau. I could make a living selling art and look for a job. But I had two warrants for my arrest with no money to get out of jai -- I would be stuck behind bars for years.

I said my tearful good-byes to the girls and my mother; and my dad and I headed down I-95. Two days later I caught a flight to Nassau.

Hindsight says I should have just faced the charges and used the money I had to work toward getting out of jail, but the power of Bipolar thoughts was strong. It honestly made sense to run and leave everything behind. In my head it all made sense, I honestly believed I was doing the only reasonable thing by running. I had been off my meds for six months, self-medicating with alcohol and sleeping pills. The voices were louder than they had ever been, and I couldn't make the distinction what my thoughts were over the volume of the other voice. In less than a year I was having my second Bipolar break.

Mother, Mother Ocean

Nassau was everything I had imagined. I found a cemetery to stash my luggage in during the day, hidden from thieves. At night I slept in my hammock on the beach, avoiding the local police. I quickly found a bar that would allow me to draw caricatures for the customers in exchange for tips. I did this for a week until I found a local place to stay for cheap.

I was able to locate a hotel that charged by the week called the Diplomat Inn. It was a nice place, with several rooms that all shared two bathrooms and a kitchen. Rum was very cheap, and it helped to quiet the voices in my head.

I was battling with manic episodes and that came with the hypersexuality. I had been spending time with a Peruvian girl who lived upstairs. It was nothing serious, just simple sex. She followed me everywhere and my Spanish was limited so our communication was limited. Sex in any language is simple.

After two weeks of going to the same bar every night, drawing caricatures of tourist I met a local named Rat. He was English and sounded like Ozzy Osbourne. He was short and blond and very loud. He was fascinated with my artwork and invited me to stay at his home for free. We drank all night and the next day I moved out of the Diplomat Inn and took a taxi to Rat's house. It was a large estate with a pool and pool house.

Rat welcomed me into his home with loving arms. He had several people living with him and I was giving the room off of his bedroom. It was a large room and all he asked was my artwork in exchange for rent. He told me the ideas he had for paintings and he wanted caricatures of his friends. This was the perfect situation for me.

I spent my days in the straw market selling watercolors and doing caricatures. I met so many interesting people and I felt alive. I was able to forget my troubles at home and just work on getting better. I was medicating with Rum and weed. I drank a bottle a day to curb the manic phases. I was making enough money to survive all the while my child support was adding up back home.

I had many adventures with Rat over the year I lived there. We made a few trips to Fort Lauderdale and Miami in Rat's boat.

From my early days in elementary school I had been obsessed with Ernest Hemingway and I shared a birthday with him. I always wanted to die the same day as him, and to live a life like his. With Rat at the helm I felt like I was living the life that Hemingway lived. Drinking all day, smoking cigars, meeting interesting people and smuggling contraband into the states from the islands.

Everyday was a different adventure in the Bahamas. Rat constantly had something under his belt, some new deal. He owned a dredging service that handled the ports and occasionally he went on trips, leaving me with the other house guest. I wasn't as liked by the other house guest because I didn't have a stable job. On one of Rat's trips I decided to move out and go live with Rat's good friend, Mikey.

Mikey lived on Ship Chanel Cay, a secluded island an hour away from Nassau. It was used by a tour company through out the week as a day trip destination. Boats of tourists would show up and the tourist would spend the day being pampered having adventures. Mikey let me work as a divemaster to take the tourists on underwater tours. My payment was free food, beer, and a place to sleep.

We took a small boat to a local marina where I could use the internet connection to email my mom and Rachel. I told them I loved them, and I was healing, but the truth was I was depressed and missed them very much.

At night on the island it was quiet, and I would go to sleep listening to my music. I dreamt of my daughters faces and my son, James. I missed them so much, but I was roughly a thousand miles away -- what kind of father was I? I started to see things for what they were. I was avoiding my role of father, spending my days in paradise while my kids lived their lives without their father. But before you save someone else, you must save yourself. I was healing daily but not in a real, therapeutic way. Being away from the problems was giving me space, but I was drowning my pain with alcohol and avoiding the depression with cocaine. I wasn't loving myself; I was slowly killing myself but instead of doing it in an old city I was doing in paradise.

I had been gone for over a year when I realized the right thing was to come home. I caught a ride with Rat to Miami on one of his regular trips to visit friends, and then said my goodbyes to him and caught a Greyhound Bus to Greenville.

I spent two days on a bus getting home, and all I had were shorts. I arrived in the middle of winter storm with a full beard and long hair. At the bus station my family walked by me twice before I stopped them and asked if they recognized me. It was good to be home, but I had a lot to deal with.

My mother arranged a visit with Rachel, knowing she wouldn't tell her mother. Seeing Rachel was the greatest moment -- it was such a relief. Unfortunately, we couldn't trust that Savannah would keep it quiet. I needed to work to pay off child support before I could turn myself in for the blackmail charges. My return home and being back in town had to be kept quiet.

I was able to stay with a family friend who understood my situation. She helped me find odd jobs to do to make money. I did this for 3 months and then tried to get Deb to drop the charges. She was very firm that she would never drop the charges. She told me she wanted me to go away for a long time and that she would try to take away any custody I had. This sent me into a depressive spiral.

I was back to the feelings of flight versus stay and work it out. I had convinced myself that I had no chance, so it was time to hit the road again. I made my plans, this time to Mexico and away for good.

I took what money I had saved and bought a ticket on a greyhound bus from Atlanta to Brownsville Texas. From Brownsville I took another bus to Matamoros, Mexico. I was able to get another bus to Playa del Carmen, Mexico. It took three days to drive across Mexico to the beaches of Carmen.

I had booked a room at *La Rana Cansada*, The Tired Frog, a simple guesthouse that rented by the week. I settled in and had enough money to stay three weeks and eat daily. I found a place to do caricatures and sell watercolor paintings. I found it harder to work there because they were stricter about work visas than the Bahamas.

I spent my days drinking heavily to remain numb. I didn't have access to cocaine, nor would I have tried. I was terrified of the thought of being arrested in Mexico. It was a scary place with lots of danger for a white tourist who strayed off the grid. Tequila and rum kept me numb and helped me make it through the nights. I missed Rachel more than I had ever missed her in the Bahamas. What little time I had spent with her had just made it worse.

I spent each day working and then paying a visit to a local Catholic church. The priest had noticed my daily visits and greeted me with a kind word. One day he approached me and asked if I would like to talk. It was the first time I had met with a priest in years.

I told him how I was running from the law, running from responsibility and I missed my children terribly. I told him how I had lived in the Bahamas and tried to come home but ended up running again.

He told me that I could run the rest of my life but no matter where I went my problems would always be waiting for me. With those words I left three days later. I knew where I belonged, and I knew what I needed to do. It was time to face my mistakes and be the dad I was meant to be. I missed my kids, my mother and father, my grandparents and I missed home. It was time to do the right thing and fight for what was mine.

Home Sweet Home

After arriving home, I made a trip to the local free clinic for mental health. Greenville Mental Health was a large facility that worked with both insured and uninsured patients as well as providing a rehabilitation service. I started seeing a local doctor who prescribed Depakote and Effexor as well as Ambien for sleep.

I was able to secure a job at MCI as a sales support operator. I was making good money and after three months was able to get caught up on my child support without alerting the authorities to my presence. My mom would pay the child support for me after I gave her my paycheck. I was able to have a stable home life, occasionally getting to see Rachel and James but never Savannah. I missed her so much, but it wasn't safe to let her know that her daddy was back in town. Rachel kept my secret and James was too young to tell.

I made several friends at MCI. One of the people I met was named Amber. She and her boyfriend spent time with me, we went to hockey games together. I was happy to socialize with other people, it made me feel normal. Amber loved how funny I was when I was manic, but she told me I needed to get control of myself. It was really the first time someone had ever said it to me that way. My new mantra was he who controls himself controls the universe. I'm still friends with Amber to this day, and I appreciate her words of wisdom.

The medication helped my depression, but my manic phases were still out of control, as well as the hypersexuality. I felt like a whore most of the time. I met women, made small talk and then ended up at their place to have sex. This happened weekly with different women. I thought about sex constantly, craved it all throughout the day. I felt guilty for focusing on anything but the mission of paying off my child support and getting my kids back. But that didn't stop me.

I worked at MCI until the local Sheriffs Department tracked my paycheck activity from my social security number back to the source and showed up to arrest me. I lost my job that day and was booked and charged with blackmail. I was housed in isolation again because of being a previous employee. I had no contact with other inmates and no meds. I was going through withdrawals from my meds, and the pain of the Bipolar flooding my unmedicated brain. All the noise and voices, all the ups and downs cycling constantly tearing at me in a 10' by 5' jail cell. I spent five days in isolation until my parents raised the money to bail me out. At least it was over, now I was no longer running or hiding from the authorities. I was out and free to exist.

My mother booked a weekend retreat with the kids and me in the mountains at a quaint little cabin. I was able to spend three days with my beautiful daughters and see my son and my parents. It felt good to be back. My mother said Rachel hadn't been so happy in over a year. Savannah had so many questions and I told her the truth. That's all I had from then on out, the truth.

I was able to get a job at a loan company that offered small loans to customers. My job was that of chaser, I went after the people who stopped paying on their loans or people who were late. Being a former detective, this was a great job for me, and it paid better than most.

So, for the first time in a long time, I was on medication, seeing a therapist, and working. I was on the road to recovery. I was proud of myself, but I could only be so comfortable knowing that I had a hearing coming up on the blackmail charges. I knew I was looking at a maximum sentence of ten years.

I decided to change doctors and go to a private practice since I had insurance. I was able to get a little more personal attention. I was looking to rid myself of the extreme manic phases, this of course meant trying out different medications. All in all, I tried about five different meds, each one making me sleepy and making it difficult to work. My doctor suggested someone as advanced as myself with Bipolar disorder go on disability. This wasn't something I had considered. But his argument was good, I had trouble working with others, the meds made it difficult to function in a work environment. He also suggested my shoulder injury from years ago would help as well.

I wanted to work as long as I could, I wanted to be as normal as I could be. Was this too much to ask? Could I ever be a functioning adult and make it in the world? How would people look at me being on disability?

Before I could really consider disability, my grandfather slipped into bad health. He found out he had lung cancer in his left lung. And just like that he was scheduled for surgery. My grandfather was like a father to me, the thought of losing him sent me into a deep depression. The night came before his surgery and I sat with him talking, recalling my childhood and how important he had been to me. He told me he was proud of me and that I was like a son to him. I left him that night and the next day he had his surgery.

My grandfather developed an infection after the surgery while in recovery and never really regained consciousness. He spent a week in the ICU and then the doctor told us it was up to family if we wanted to keep him on life support.

It was the hardest decision we ever made but he wouldn't have wanted to be on life support. I held his head, my grandmother and mother on either side of him and we turned off the machine that was keeping him alive. He faded off quickly and just like that the man I idolized was gone. He had been a source of constant enlightenment. My whole life he guided me in the direction I needed to go. Even when I strayed off track, I knew the direction I needed to head because of his guidance.

We buried him in April 2004. Two weeks later I had my hearing. I was at a crossroads in my life. I had just lost my closest friend, and the way he died had left its mark on me. He was a preacher, like his father before him. A man of God, who in my opinion had never sinned. He was a model citizen and the perfect Christian. I idolized him and knew I could never be anything like him. I knew the minute he died that I could never believe in God again. I became an atheist the day he died. How could a God make his most loyal servant suffer like that at his death? My grandfather was such a holy man and he had been off cigarettes for 30 years and then just develops cancer. It made no sense to me, but regardless I was through with the idea of a higher entity controlling things. It was just us humans floating in a universe with no direction. Whatever happened, happened.

That was the day I became an atheist. I had concluded that no god could ever give a baby brain cancer and no god could ever take away a holy devout man in such a painful way. I refused to accept that God worked in mysterious ways. As far as I was concerned, I had been lied to my entire life and mislead by people too blind to realize that God was a lie.

My hearing came on a Wednesday and I knew there was a good chance I would be going to prison. I was embarrassed as the attorney read off my charges and told the judge what I had done. I plead guilty and asked for leniency, I stated that I knew what I did was wrong, and I was very sorry of causing my ex wife any pain and suffering for my idiotic behavior. The judge thought about it for a few minutes and then said, "ten-year suspended sentence, three years' probation and $10,000 in fines." I had never been so scared in my life, but it was over.

A Fresh Start

After my grandfather's death and my trial, I decided to move in with my grandmother. She was alone and needed the help around the house. I had been transferred to another loan location, because of a one-night stand with the secretary of the office. I would still be doing the same job of collections. At this point I was on board with my doctor with going on disability. I found it increasingly difficult to work with others and no matter what time I took my pills I was always hung over. There was one employee that always pushed my buttons and as much as I tried, I couldn't escape his harassment. He accused me of being high and questioned my work ethic. I wasn't open to explaining my mental health to him or anyone else. My manager knew about my situation and gave me certain freedoms. I found myself sleeping in my car when I was supposed to be out chasing customers. I drank so much coffee that I had the jitters and an upset stomach.

I finally lost control one day when my coworker was relentlessly giving me a hard time. I had fallen asleep at my desk and he was convinced I was on drugs. He demanded our manager fire me, but the manager stood up for me. I became so mad and out of control I picked up a chair and threw it through the window. Then I locked myself in the bathroom. An hour later my dad came and picked me up and took me to the doctor's office.

I was able to go on medical leave for a few weeks and then the company decided to let me go. I was caught up on child support and my grandmother was helping with my expenses. I had been doing my artwork on the side, selling a few paintings here and there so I decided to pursue my artwork under the table. I had applied for my disability and they told me I couldn't have a job during the application process. My music and my art kept me busy. I spent my days painting and at night I practiced guitar, catching up on all the years I just played for fun.

I was able to get some mural jobs at local schools. The money was good, and I enjoyed being around the children. Word got around about my murals and I had several schools lined up. I could come and go as I pleased, working on my schedule, and I could put on headphones and escape while listening to music. I didn't have to interact with others or answer to a boss. It was the perfect job for me.

It still hurt knowing that I only had visitation with my children, I longed for more interaction in their lives. Their mother controlled everything, and I was never kept in the loop. I usually found out things from Rachel.

I made it a point to speak to the children daily on the phone. One day I was unable to get them, I called their home and nothing. I tried their mothers cell phone and still nothing. I was worried about my children, so I called Debs father and he told me it was none of my business. After arguing for several minutes, he told me they were in Florida. Our court agreement forbids leaving the state without notifying the other parent. He told me I wasn't their father anymore and I needed to leave them alone. I blacked out and started trashing my grandmothers house. When I came to my hand was bleeding from smashing a picture frame. I was no longer insured and was unable to see my regular doctor so the next day my dad took me back to Greenville Mental Health.

The doctors felt my condition had worsened and they needed to put me on something much stronger. They started me on Lithium. This was the standard for more advanced Bipolar symptoms. Lithium had been around for years and originally used for heart conditions. It took a few weeks before it got into my system and the levels were where they needed to be, but I was calmer and more evened out.

I was on Lithium for my Bipolar Disorder and Seroquel for sleep. I became violent if someone tried to wake me from sleep while on the Seroquel. It became a rule in the house that nobody was to touch me while I was sleeping. The Lithium caused weight gain, pushing my weight up an extra 20 lbs. The Lithium also caused heavy urination, and I always felt dehydrated. I had to learn to drink a lot more water daily and stay out of the sun.

The disability process was painful. I went through meetings with the Social Security doctors and filled out forms and answered questions. We waited an entire year to find out I had been turned down. They told us to appeal it with an attorney. So, we hired an attorney and went through the entire process again. Another year passed and I was able to finish my probation and be a free man.

It took two years waiting on disability before my hearing. I was awarded disability during the hearing and began the process of waiting for the money to come in. Of course, the attorney got his share first then I received a back-pay amount. I decided I wanted to pursue my music full time and join a band. I needed better gear, so I took part of my back-pay and went to Guitar Center.

Now that I had a steady check coming in, I could focus my energy on my music. I bought a recording setup and started creating. It helped with the noise in my head and gave me something to do besides lay on the couch all day and being depressed.

Practicing eight hours a day had started to pay off, I was secure enough in my musical abilities to start looking for bands. Every week I had a different audition with a different band.

As my grandmother got older my mother decided it would be best if we were to move in with her. So, my grandmother and I packed up our belongings and moved in with my parents. They purchased a new home in a new community, and I had twice as much room.

I had been single for several years and I really wanted to settle down again and get married, but I felt like I had little to offer. I was a disabled, up and coming musician who did school murals. I didn't have a big income and I struggled from month to month. I had three kids and I lived with my parents. None of this was attractive, but I decided to try Match.com.

After about two months online I found a young lady in the city of Greenwood that popped out. She was an exotic beauty, with features that looked Hispanic or Native American. Tanned skin and dark hair and a beautiful body. I was taken by this person. I was in love with her at first site. I thought that was the Bipolar talking but none the less I wanted to meet her. So, I sent her a message.

We hit it off immediately and had so much in common. She was enticed by my stories of the islands and she loved that I was a musician. We met in May and waited until June to have our first date. I wanted it to be special, so I planned on June sixth, 2006 as our first date. 06/06/06 wouldn't happen again for another thousand years. Our first date we met at her house and spent the entire night curled up in each other's arms. It was a magical night, but I was so afraid that I would ruin it somehow because of my Bipolar Disorder.

I knew after our first date that I wanted to marry her. I had never felt so in love with someone. It was completely different from Deborah and Tonja. It felt natural and I really cared about her. I knew that it wasn't a Bipolar obsession, it was different. I couldn't explain it, but I knew that I wanted to be with her for the rest of my life.

We continued to see each other. I wrote a long letter to her explaining my mental illness, my situation with my children and my history with the law. I wanted full disclosure and if she rejected me at least I knew I had been honest. I waited a day for her response, to which she replied that she understood, and it changed nothing.

Angie and I met in May of 2006 and were married in November of 2006. We were very happy together and she was very accepting of my condition. For the first time in years I was truly happy. It took time for her to get use to my children and my family, but she did a great job fitting in.

Over the next few years I became more successful with my music, joining several bands and illustrating children's books. But my Bipolar was getting worse. I was suicidal and hypersexual, and becoming increasingly difficult to deal with. I kept to myself and didn't open up to Angie what was going on. The voices were so loud, and I made bad decisions constantly.

Marriage was two people working together and I was not holding up my end of things. I fought with Angie over just about everything. The kids were stuck in the middle and saw firsthand how I was suffering. It took a toll on Rachel. She began using drugs and cutting herself. Years of pain and repressed emotion had worn Rachel down, and she needed help.

We found Rachel on the cold floor of our garage unconscious one late night. She had gone out to smoke after taking a large amount of drugs. She was transported to the hospital via ambulance and given charcoal. After she came to, she was admitted into the Carolina Behavioral Center for teens. She spent two weeks there before being moved to another hospital in Columbia, where she was diagnosed with Borderline Personality Disorder. After a few weeks she was released and moved in with Angie and me.

The feeling that I somehow had something to do with my child's mental condition was saddening. My genetics surely had something to do with my daughter's diagnosis. I fully expected the doctors to return with a Bipolar Diagnosis, and the to be honest I had never heard of BPD. But the diagnosis description fit her so well. Had I caused this by cheating on her mother? Did my absence manifest this disorder? How could I have done this to my precious daughter? She was my best friend, the best man at my wedding and now I had done something so horrible. It would have been easier if the finger could point at me, but it wasn't that easy. Genetically there was a chance that she would have some sort of mental disorder based on my Bipolar Disorder. My father's father was an alcoholic, so I was more likely to be an addict or have addictive qualities. It was a cross that I had to bear.

I was happy being married to Angie; she was the perfect wife. Being a nurse, she was able to understand my mental disorder and know that I never purposely acted different. It was something that I had no control over, the ups and downs. But she was also human, and she could only take so much. The hypersexuality was difficult in many ways. As a partner I was demanding, sex was expected whenever I wanted it. It went from being something we shared to something I demanded.

On two occasions Angie caught me sexting with two separate women. This crushed her and nearly cost me my marriage. I still don't understand how she could have ever forgiven me. It was an inexcusable action on my part. I was addicted to the rush of talking to these other women, the thought of being caught. I said things to them I didn't mean, made promises I had no desire to fulfill. Would I have taken it further and actually met them? Would I have destroyed my marriage the way I destroyed my first marriage? The difference was that deep down inside I loved Angie, she was my world. I honestly don't think it could have ever gone past sexting, but I was being driven an invisible force.

Hypersexuality is defined as Sexual addiction or as a dysfunctional preoccupation with sexual fantasy, often in combination with the obsessive pursuit of casual or non-intimate sex; pornography; compulsive masturbation; romantic intensity and objectified partner sex for a period of at least six months. (1)

My entire adult life I have been obsessed with sexual encounters. Starting at a young age I have been obsessed with females. The smell of their hair, their faces and their bodies. It was like climbing a mountain, the challenge was to get to the top and plant the flag. I looked at women as a mission, do everything in your power to make her yours. Being married took that mission away. She was mine; I didn't need to conquer her and make her mine. She was mine, in body and soul. So, the act of sex was a merely an act. There was no chase or mission. It was a simple act of kissing, hugging and moving toward the bedroom. This was not to say sex wasn't great, it was. I was a very inventive lover, but the chase was nowhere to be found. That was the allure of sexting with strangers. But these ladies were obtainable and the things I said to them could have been understood to mean that I really wanted a relationship with them.

It was a long process of healing and proving myself to Angie. I had to earn her trust again. My computer and phone became open to inspection at any time and there was no more lying. I truly wanted to make it work, I understood where I went wrong and I needed to make it right. Nobody had ever hurt Angie like I hurt her, and I needed to fix this. I truly loved her and couldn't stand what I had done.

It was around 2014 I became friends with Bob. Bob and I started a band called Contra Blues Band. Bob was 20 years my senior and looked at me like a son, and at times a brother. We grew very close and he took it upon himself to help me with my disorder. I learned that Bob suffered from Multiple Myeloma, a cancer in the bone marrow. He and I grew close very fast and he helped me through many of my manic episodes. He kept me on target, focused on getting better and controlling myself.

Bob and I had many concerts together, we were a brotherhood, but our friendship wasn't just on stage. Bob knew I was suicidal; he could see through my jokes. It was easier to joke about wanting to kill myself than to breakdown and confess to my love ones that I really wanted to die. And it wasn't so much that I wanted to die, it was more that I just didn't want to live. Living was painful, life was hard and full of heartbreak. I felt everything so deeply, from Angie to my kids, to the words of a song. It all hit me so hard. I cried at the drop of a hat and spent my time sleeping through the pain.

Shortly after I met Bob I was diagnosed with Psoriatic Arthritis. I had physical pain constantly and took pain pills daily. Shortly after my diagnosis I was prescribed Lyrica. I was taking a cocktail of Lyrica, Tramadol, Lithium, and Ambien. I was constantly high from the medications. And when the Bipolar got too bad I took too much tramadol and Ambien and I would pass out for a day or two. Every time I did this, I scared Angie to death. She lived in constant fear that I would accidentally overdose and kill myself. I would black out and say things on Facebook or start fights with Angie and the next day have no clue what I had done. I was spiraling out of control.

Much like my time in college, I would get scared from my near-death experiences and go sober for a week or two. I would stop taking the pills with alcohol or give up alcohol all together. I would do this for months at a time. I never had such an addiction to alcohol that I craved it daily, it was more of a tool to zone out when things got too bad, when things were so painful that I couldn't cope.

I stayed with Contra Blues Band for three years before leaving to form Widow Lake with a female singer named Angela. She and I had known each other for several years and she promised if her band ever broke up, she would start something with me.

Widow Lake took off quickly and for the first time I felt like a real rock star. When we were on stage, I felt like I was sharing the spotlight with Angela. She and I had a great thing with this band and we both knew it. We quickly became the biggest thing in town, other local bands flocked to see us. A female fronted hard rock band was a rare thing in this town, and it was a much-welcomed attraction. My ego thrived on stage and it always seemed to be that I had a manic episode when we had a concert. When I was lacking in energy there was always coffee and energy drinks. No more cocaine for me, I had learned my lesson.

I felt like my family life had started to fray. Rachel had moved to New Orleans and developed a nasty heroin addiction. She was able to get checked into a rehab facility. Savannah was diagnosed as Bipolar and my nanny was starting to have health issues.

Losing Rachel took a huge toll on me. She gave no warning, she just up and moved to New Orleans. We had started slipping away from one another. She became distant and started socializing with people I just didn't approve of. She had dropped out of college and moved to Spartanburg, a town outside of Greenville. And then one day she called and said she had moved to New Orleans. This was a major stressor for me, and I started using more and more pain pills and alcohol. The pain was too much at times.

I tried to focus on home and the things around me. Mostly helping Savannah learn to cope with Bipolar Disorder. She had moved in with Angie and me. I had never been around another Bipolar person before Savannah came to live with us. I didn't know what to expect, but we didn't have the same types of Bipolar. Savannah was more down, and I was more manic. She was able to work, and I made my way playing on the streets between concerts. We both had direction and focus in our lives, but our emotions controlled us.

One night I sat at the table in the kitchen, after taking pain pills and spilled my guts to Angie. I finished off a bottle of whiskey while telling her how the loss of Rachel had torn a hole in my heart so large that it was pulling in everything. I felt like my world was collapsing. All I ever thought about was dying and ridding myself of pain. She sat there crying watching her husband dying in front of her. And she could do nothing to help. I passed out and that was all of that for now. I tucked it down deep and put on a happy face. I had my band fooled, the only people I ever talked to was my friends, Bob and Jim. They heard me talk about the depression but always with a joke to lessen the severity of it. Jim was suffering from depression, so he knew all too well how bad it hurt. They didn't know it but there were days that our brief conversations kept me alive, it gave me perspective. How could I be so down when Bob was facing death from cancer and Jim was battling depression. I felt selfish and hated myself for being that way.

There were days I woke up late and made my way to the couch and turned on YouTube. I would listen to Ed Sheeran or Lifehouse on the down days or Kelly Clarkson on the up days. Music helped to shape my daily moods. It was therapeutic. It was much more helpful than my doctor. Over the years I had seen many doctors from older ladies to an Asian doctor that I could never understand to a young doctor who helped me get my disability to the doctor I had at this time. He was an older man who wore a lab coat and never looked at me. He focused on his computer, typing the entire visit. The words, "I wanna die", never phased him. He just kept writing. I really felt like I could have sliced my wrist in the office, and he would just keep writing. I even thought about doing it once. If I was going to get better, I had to find another doctor.

For anyone that has ever been through the pain of finding a new doctor, it's common knowledge that you don't find a doctor, your insurance company dictates who you go to. I wanted someone young, preferably a male for my psychiatrist and a female for my counselor. Angie brought home a list of the doctors that were covered under our plan and I chose two from the list. It took me a while to actually call because there was always a hesitation about changing doctors. You are faced with the possibility of changing your meds or picking someone who is wrong straight out of the chute. Every time I have ever changed doctors it has affected me in some way or another. Unfortunately, you can't sample your doctor and tell if they are someone you can connect with, someone you feel comfortable with.

I chose a young doctor named Dr. Jason Flassing and a counselor named Roxie Medlin. I had high hopes for both, and I wasn't disappointed. It was an instant connection with Dr. Flassing and Roxie. It made it easier that I got along with them and I seemed to honestly matter to them. I hadn't been so happy with my doctor and counselor before. Clicking with your doctor and counselor is a first step toward positive healthcare.

On the home front, things had become to difficult for Savannah to continue to live with us -- I was too out of control and there was a conflict between our personalities. So, she moved home to live with her mother. I was sad to see her go but deep down I understood. I could barely stand to be around me. Savannah and I had become like to opposing magnets, although she loved me very much, I had begun to lose myself even more.

On February 4th, 2018 my nanny passed away. This was one of the final straws on the camels back. I was down on my knees trying to cope with life and now the woman who raised me as a child was gone. It was a monthly date for me and my nanny to go shopping when she got her social security check. We always went out to eat and bought her groceries. She laughed and had fun with me. I spent as much time with her as possible. I had lived with her for two years after my grandfather had passed away. We were closer than I had ever been with any family. To say I would miss her was an injustice, I was torn. First, I lost Rachel and now my nanny was gone. I honestly didn't want to live anymore.

I honestly felt like I had a hole in my life. It was a black hole that sucked out all energy and light. I tried to explain when a Bipolar person loses someone its many times harder than a normal person losing someone. Everything we feel is exaggerated and multiplied compared to the average person. I was mourning the death of my grandmother and the loss of my daughter. It seemed harder with Rachel because she was alive, and she was living nine hours from home. I could talk to her but not feel her presence. It was an empty hole that I could not fill.

My counselor suggested I put myself into my music and focus on that. I tried but it was difficult working with the band. I had personal differences with the drummer, and we argued constantly. He would say the most horrible things to me and then apologize. One moment he would say we were brothers and the next he was telling me off. Was this what it was like to live with me, was this how Bipolar was?

I could never be open and up front to my bandmates about what I really was going through. I always feared they would fire me for being so unstable, so I learned to cover it up. I would ride the manic episodes and be funny, and the depressed phases were always camouflaged by energy drinks. When I was depressed, I was just quiet, so they chalked it up to me being moody.

One fateful day things got heated during a group texting and I had taken enough abuse from the drummer, so I quit. I think I was more hurt that the other band mates didn't defend me. I expected more from them, but even when the drummer was saying the cruelest things they never came to my defense. So that was it, I threw away a band that I co-founded and worked hard to make into a money maker. I gave it all up because I could no longer be strong, I was at a breaking point. To this day, I still regret not fighting for what was mine, giving up comes so easy. To just walk away and not experience whatever emotions happen. Its easier to avoid a myriad of emotions and just quit.

I had gotten to a place in my depression that I was seeking out ways to die. My last attempt had somewhat failed. I was able to be revived and I didn't want that to happen again. I found a website that gave pill combinations and directions for ending your suffering. I had quite the collections of pills from my pain management doctor as well as plenty of sleeping pills. It wasn't that my doctor and counselor weren't working I just wasn't telling them how bad it really was. I refused to open up for fear that the doctor would commit me. I wasn't ready at that moment to confess how bad it really was or to give in and get help. I was moody and distant from Angie and everyone knew I was bad off, but nobody could do anything about it. I rarely talked to my friends or my family.

Angie and I got into a nasty fight one night and she said something harsh about Rachel. I became aggressive and pushed her down, and I saw how frightened she was of me. My aggression had always been dangerous but never directed at her. I was out of control; I remember just seeing colors and reacting to her. I would never have hurt her, but this had gone too far. She was angry and scared. What was I doing? I was secretly planning to kill myself, going as far as to have a bottle of pills in my studio. I was pushing my wife down and losing control. This was the very last straw. The very last one.

Angie distanced herself from me and sought help for her depression at the Carolina Behavioral Hospital. I watched Savannah and Angie both go through day programs to help them. I watched them transform into stronger women. I wanted this, I wanted to get better so bad, I was so tired of wanting to die. Angie was better every day. She came home from the hospital and shared what she learned, and I listened, wanting to be better myself. I watched the color come back into her life and I loved the new her. She was learning boundaries and grounding exercises. But was this something I could do? It was a big step for me, but so was suicide. It had come down to one or the other.

Around this time, I had an appointment with Dr. Flassing. I told him how the voices were so loud in my head. I told him how I just wanted it to be quiet. There was so much noise in my head and the ever-present voice just persisted on making things worse. It was so difficult to focus with all the noise. He prescribed Geodon and within 5 days the voice was gone. I really didn't know how to feel about this. On one hand it was nice to not hear the constant talking but on the other hand this voice was my closest friend. He had been with me since childhood. I was on the wall about it. I missed him, as weird as it sounds, he was my friend. He gave me bad advice and was horribly deceptive but nonetheless he was my friend. How could you go 45 years with a voice in your head and not become attached? I felt like I had murdered my friend.

So much was changing, and I needed to come clean with Angie about everything. About my pill stash and about losing the voice. I needed help and she was going to be the first one to know.

I sat down with Angie and told her about my bottle of pills and how I had a suicide note written and ready to go. All it would take was one dramatic episode and I would end it. I was closer than I had been since 2002. She didn't want to lose me, and I loved her. I never wanted to hurt my family and I was on the verge. We both agreed I needed help. But I wanted to go out in true fashion as I did everything.

I scheduled a small concert, and without using the words farewell show, I performed my last show for a while. I needed a break from music, from the world of music. I needed a break from the people who called themselves my friends and from the things that tore me down daily. I needed a break from mourning for Rachel and Nanny. I needed to fix myself. I performed the concert on a Friday night to small intimate crowd and then that Saturday I packed my bags and checked myself into the Carolina Behavioral Hospital.

The program was a full stay program. This meant no cell phones, no shoelaces, no drawstrings and you followed a strict schedule of therapy and meetings. It was overwhelming at first. I panicked at the thought of being without simple things like pens and caffeine. I voluntarily checked myself in, so why did I have to adhere to such insane rules? As with everything I fought what I disagreed with. But I acclimated and calmed down. It took me a day to relax and finally I was able to make friends. My room mate was Bipolar as well and we got along well. We talked at night until we both passed out from the medication. During the day I learned coping exercises and the discipline to put myself first.

There were group meetings constantly from the early morning to late at night. We did everything as a group. Some of the people were worse off than me and others not quite as bad. Some were there from failed suicide attempts, some from a need to become sober. We all had our stories and our reasons for needing help. Having been locked up I think that this was a far cry from incarceration. We had freedom but it was limited. After five days it was my turn to meet with the doctors to decide my fate.

Meeting with the hospital doctors I was told about Electroconvulsive Therapy. They explained it was once known as Electroshock Therapy. I knew all about this from my obsession with Ernest Hemingway. He had undergone Electroshock Therapy at the Mayo Clinic before his death. He felt it destroyed his ability to write. But the doctor told me ECT was safer and less invasive. She explained that you were put under with anesthesia and given a short flow of electricity into your brain. She told me it could completely do away with my desire to kill myself. This was very appealing to me. I couldn't imagine what it was like to live without wanting to die. I had lived everyday since I was 16 wanting in someway or another to end my life.

I was given a day to talk to Angie about it and then report back to the doctor what I wanted to do. I called Angie and told her the good news. All I could see was life without wanting to die. She of course was apprehensive about such a drastic procedure. I was determined that this is what I wanted to do. I needed to do it.'

The first step was to go off the Lyrica and the Lithium because of their reactions with the procedure. This was easier said than done. Coming straight off the Lyrica was like going cold turkey from Heroin. I was terribly sick to my stomach, vomiting and have severe cramps. I felt like I was drugged, I had no energy at all. I was dismissed from the hospital and scheduled to come back for my first session of ECT on that Friday. I was unable to make it because I was so sick. They rescheduled it for the following Monday. It took me a month to completely come off the Lyrica.

That Monday I arrived at 8:30 am and was taken to a hospital bed. I was given an IV and a bag of saline and had a monitor hooked up to me. They walked me through the process. It was a line of patients waiting to go into "the room". This room was behind two doors and it connected to a recovery room. It was a continuous flow of patients. Finally, it was my turn. I was given a mouth guard to bite on and then an oxygen mask was placed over my face. The anesthesia was given, and I was out. I remember waking up to a strange haunting noise and trying to focus. I was in the recovery room and I could feel something in my hair. It was the gel they put on your head for the ECT device to deliver the current into your brain. I was out of things for a few minutes. They wheeled me back to the waiting area and when I could walk, they had me sit in a chair and checked my vitals before discharging me.

I rode home with Angie, confused and blinded by the bright light. I just wanted to go home and crash on the couch. The whole ordeal had exhausted me. But I was convinced that the doctors knew what was best and were guiding me in the right direction.

I'd be lying if I said I could remember all the ECT sessions. One of the side effects of ECT is loss of memory. Most of what I do remember is a blur. I made it through seven sessions and decided that was enough. I felt like anymore and I would lose me. Its very difficult to describe but the ECTs made me unsteady on my feet, unsure about everyday decisions and confused in general. I don't know how much of these feelings had to do with anesthesia or if it was all the ECT. Every session I lost a little more of who I was.

Some of the side effects I noticed were a change in my palette; food didn't taste the same. I found that I could no longer eat oatmeal, even after eating it every day for breakfast for years. Bread was another thing I couldn't stomach. Smells were also different. One of the worst side effects was my loss of interest in my music. I went months without picking up my guitar for the pure desire of doing it. I forced myself to play weekly just to keep up my finger strength.

Angie noticed even more differences in me. She said that my breath was different, and she saw me as a stranger. This became the topic of several arguments between us. She hated the idea of ECT, but I no longer wanted to kill myself. That part of me was gone. I reasoned that no matter how much harm it had done, ECT saved my life. But at what cost? I was quiet all the time and I had ceased having manic episodes.

Over a two-month period I received seven ECT sessions, and in that time, I went from a manic episode daily to no manic episodes at all. I went from being talkative to sitting in silence for hours at a time. My entire palette had changed, foods I loved I now hated. I also noticed that my OCD had subsided, and I no longer obsessed over order and cleanliness.

My doctor told me it would take a year before I started to get back to my old self. He told me it was normal after ECT to fill outside of myself. Now I simply found myself depressed. I had gone from Bipolar to Depressed in a matter of months. It would be difficult to transition to this new life.

Ten months had passed, and I was adjusting to the new me. I no longer had suicidal thoughts or tendencies. I was depressed daily, unable to find the drive to play my music or do anything other than sit on the couch and watch television. I watched the same cartoons over and over. I basically forced myself to eat meals, not enjoying the food in general. I had been playing music with a friend of mine, doing a couple of concerts a month but that was the extent of my music interactions. I didn't obsess over the guitar; I didn't feel the passion and drive I once felt so deeply. I had lost interest in sex and basic communication was a chore. I learned so much about myself during this time. I learned that my entire life had been driven by manic episodes, manic episodes that I didn't have anymore. All the passion and drive in my life had come from those bursts of energy that had infected me from childhood up until the ECT.

Almost a year after I had been hospitalized, I found myself in a deep depression. Even though there were no suicidal thoughts I felt incapable of functioning from day to day. I slept in until noon, and then spent the rest of the day watching cartoons. I had to force myself to shower or play guitar.

I craved a manic episode; it had been so long without them. I had small manic phases once or twice, but they were more like small hyper phases that lasted about an hour. Nothing compared to the legendary manic phases that lasted for days.

I tried to enroll in a Transcranial Magnetic Stimulation (TMS) program that has had promising results for people like me, but my insurance turned me down because I am diagnosed as Bipolar instead of Major Depressive Disorder.

Depression is an ever-present monster that sometimes hides and lies dormant but must be fought daily. It's up to me to fight daily to get out of bed and be a functional adult. It's my mission to eat good foods and surround myself with positivity and avoid things that can pull me down into the depths of depression.

A year after ECT I have worked diligently with my counselor to develop a game plan for fighting my depression. It involves looking at my music differently and having goals to accomplish. It involves time at the gym and changing my diet. I need to accomplish certain things daily. Getting out of bed, showering and eating are but a few of the things I must accomplish. I live in hopes that one day my manic phases will return but until they do, I must make the best out of my situation. I can sit in depression and do nothing or take control of my life and make a difference. That's my choice. This is where I am at.

Summary

Forty-Seven years of being Bipolar has taught me many things. I've learned the importance of family and honesty. I've learned to treasure the times you have with those you love. But the most important thing I've learned about my Bipolar Disorder is when to get help. Looking back on my life I see how I needed to check myself into the hospital several times. I could have avoided so much pain and suffering if I had only checked myself into a hospital. Doctors and counselors can only do so much outside of the hospital. They don't have the ability to observe you over a 24-hour period. They can't alter your meds from day to day. That's what hospitalization is for. I've learned that you should never be afraid to seek the help that can keep you alive.

One of the most important things that you can do daily is monitor and listen to your moods. Learn to read where your mood is taking you. You can manipulate your mood to bring yourself up or down if you catch it soon enough. Using calming techniques or music you can help direct your mood. For example, if you wake up feeling down, it's possible to surround yourself with music that is more upbeat to direct your mood to stabilize or go up. In other words, if you're down when you get up in the morning and you listen to slow, depressing music you will either stay depressed or go farther down.

I use caffeine, cartoons and music to alter my mood when I am down. This is what I refer to as my secret bag of tricks. It allows me to put myself in a different mood than if I do nothing at all. Learn to listen to signals that allow you to see a mood coming -- a sudden drop in your mood lets you know your going into a depressive state. Putting yourself in your happy place can help you alter that mood enough to avoid an extreme depressive state.

Manic phases are usually harder to manipulate. Putting on soft music, sad songs or television shows that maintain a low-key mood can help you bring a manic phase down to manageable level.

This isn't always reliable, but it does work, and can you help you feel in control of an out of control situation.

One of the best ways to manage Bipolar Disorder is to have friends and family that understand you. Explaining to your friends and family that you feel everything during your depressive episodes, and you are completely out of control during manic phases can help them react to you better. A well-informed friend or family member can help you manage your moods. Its difficult to express what you feel but once they know what to look for it can help both parties to work through a difficult time.

Having a game plan is also very helpful. For example, if you feel a major depressive mood coming on being able to redirect your days events can be very useful. Working it out ahead of time with employers and friends and family can save hours of explaining your situation when you don't feel like talking. Have a plan of attack in place. Know that when the mood is coming, you need to be in your favorite chair, with a favorite snack or blanket watching your go-to show. If listening to music helps, then create a playlist before hand to listen to during your mood to help stabilize you.

If your people understand that you can't function during a bad day it makes it easier to simple say, "I'm having a bad day don't expect anything from me today."

Much more involved is creating a safe place for you to live in. I couldn't make it through each day without my safe place. My safe place is my home. When the depression is so intense, and I feel the pain of living, I turn to my surroundings. Around my house I have little displays of my favorite things, things that make me feel safe. I have a collection of action figures, a Jimi Hendrix collection, an Ernest Hemingway collection, paintings in each room that mean something special and I also have a television in almost all the major rooms. I try to avoid sitting in silence, I either have music, music videos or cartoons playing all day long. I sleep to cartoons at night, constantly manipulating my mood. I put myself in a safe zone the minute I walk through my door, far away from the real world.

There are probably doctors that would be wary of this technique -- my current doctor is aware of it and has no issues with it. For a Bipolar person the real world is full of unpredictability and can be less than kind. I know that no matter what happens outside of my home I can come home and be surrounded with my happiness.

I also have a secret "bag" of 5 things that always bring me up. I know that anywhere I am I can play my favorite artist's music and it helps me. I always have my phone with me, just like every other American alive today, and I can access my cartoons, my music, my comic books, videos and photos. I suggest creating your bag of 5 things and sharing that with your spouse or emergency contact. In the event of a break they can assist you with those things.

One of the hardest things about being Bipolar is being married. Most marriages don't last, ending after one too many breaks or major episodes. I know that my marriage has been tested and continues to be tested. My wife has stood by me through my worst and has seen me at my lowest and my highest. She's been the target of my rage and been tormented through years of me when I needed help the most. She's seen me through hospitalization and ECT. I consider myself lucky to have such a devoted and caring spouse, but I know the pain this life has caused her. I know the times that I didn't think we would make it another year together. Bipolar has been a horrible mistress but my wife is there for me. We make it work with communication. Sometimes, she must drag it out of me, but discussing what I'm going through daily helps. She knows the signs of a depressive break and knows how to avoid me when I'm manic. Its all about learning the signs.

What it comes down to is control. Knowing you can't control your Bipolar episodes, but you can do little things to alter your moods and direct how it flows. Think of it like a big wave surfer. The surfer knows where to paddle out, where to sit to catch the wave, when to paddle for the wave and when to bail. The wave is your Bipolar Disorder, and you are the surfer. You will learn what a manic episode feels like before it happens. This gives you enough time to prepare for it. This might mean changing your daily plans, avoiding certain locations or people. The surfer knows how to read the face of the wave to get the most out of the ride. Knowing your moods can allow you to avoid overspending, saying things that you regret, having unexpected sexual experiences, or overeating. We all experience our moods differently, but some things are the same. Manic phases cause us to do things we normally wouldn't do, and depressive episodes take the life out of everything.

Grounding is a commonly used practice for calming down during episodes. Finding a place to be quiet and focus, you can use grounding to make it through the hardest episodes. The 5,4,3,2,1 method is one of the most successful methods of grounding.

5 – things you can see (you can look within the room and out of the window)

4 – things you can feel (the silkiness of your skin, the texture of the material on your chair, what does your hair feel like? What is in front of you that you can touch? A table perhaps?)

3 – things you can hear (traffic noise or birds outside, when you are quiet and actually listening things in your room constantly make a noise but typically, we don't hear them).

2 – things you can smell (hopefully nothing awful!)

1 – thing you can taste (it might be a good idea to keep a piece of chocolate handy in case you are doing this grounding exercise! You can always leave your chair for this one and when you taste whatever it is that you have chosen, take a small bite and let it swill around your mouth for a couple of seconds, really savoring the flavor). (4)

Another grounding technique is to carry an object with you in your pocket that you can feel and touch, something to take your focus from the episode. A piece of cloth, a rock, a small toy, or whatever you can carry comfortably in your pocket. Hold it in your hand and run your fingers along the edges.

There are many techniques that you can learn from a hospital stay or various books. But the important thing is to be equipped with these techniques before your next episode. Be prepared.

Bipolar Disorder is never easy but with family and friends, coping techniques, knowledge and a desire to make it through each day you can get through this.

Altering your diet can help alter your Serotonin. Serotonin is believed to act as a mood stabilizer, it also produces healthy sleep patterns as well as boosting your mood. Serotonin is synthesized from tryptophan. There are several foods that can naturally increase your Serotonin.

1. Eggs

2. Cheese

3. Pineapple

4. Tofu

5. Salmon

6. Nuts and Seeds

7. Turkey

These foods can all help increase your Serotonin levels. (5) In addition to Serotonin, Vitamin D is a great way to help stabilize your mood. 10 – 15 minutes of sun per day or taking a Vitamin D supplement can help. Eating healthy and taking supplements is a great way to help your body and mind.

In conclusion, Bipolar Disorder can be managed with medication and healthy living as well as coping techniques. It requires help from friends and family as well as learning to read your moods. Regardless how long you have been living with Bipolar Disorder you can begin to manage it at any time. But it takes dedication. Utilizing your friends, family, or spouse can be an important step, but it requires full disclosure of your condition. Coping techniques take time to learn and practice but they can help you through the toughest times. Life is worth living and you are an important part of this world. It takes time and patience, but in the end its worth the effort. Never be embarrassed to share with someone that you suffer from Bipolar

Disorder, it can make things easier for you.

(1) https://psychcentral.com/lib/hypersexuality-symptoms-of-sexual-addiction/
(2) https://www.mayoclinic.org/tests-procedures/transcranial-magnetic-stimulation/about/pac-20384625
(3) https://www.healthline.com/health/adhd/history
(4) https://drsarahallen.com/7-ways-to-calm/
(5) https://www.healthline.com